Speaking and Listening

Chatting Cheetahs and Jumping Jellyfish

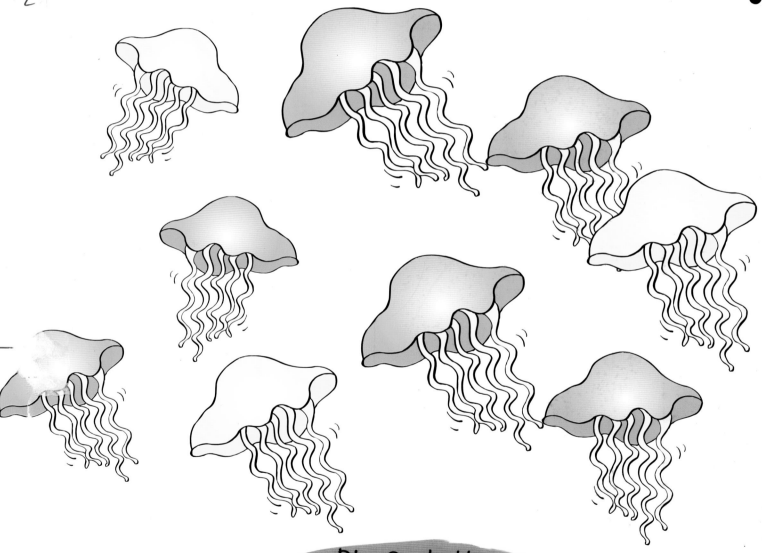

Pie Corbett and Ruth Thomson

Chrysalis Children's Books

First published in the UK in 2004 by
Chrysalis Children's Books
An imprint of Chrysalis Books Group Plc
The Chrysalis Building,
Bramley Road,
London, W10 6SP

Paperback edition first published in 2005

ISBN 1 84138 966 8 (hb)
ISBN 1 84458 312 0 (pb)

British Library Cataloguing in Publication Data
for this book is available from the British Library.

Editorial manager: Joyce Bentley
Editor: Nicola Edwards
Designers: Rachel Hamdi, Holly Mann
Illustrators: Jan McCafferty, Bridget MacKeith,
Mike Spoor and Gwyneth Williamson

Printed in China

Contents

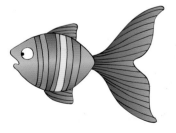

Speaking and listening

Talking helps children to think, communicate and make sense of the world around them. Children's speech flourishes where there are interesting activities to talk about. This happens through everyday activities, discussing what is happening around them, looking at interesting objects and books and talking about events at home or in school. Recounting what the family or class has done and inventing stories together are helpful ways to develop talk and the imagination. Saying funny sentences, inventing rhymes and singing are also important.

Come and have a look at this tasty book!

About this book

This book is designed for adults (whether teachers, parents or carers) and children to talk about together. It is brimming with activities that will give children opportunities to talk out loud, to develop their abilities to speak in a wide variety of ways and to listen carefully.

The activities

Each double page has a particular focus (see the contents page) and most are completely self-contained. You can open the book at any page, talk together about what you see in the detailed pictures and go backwards or forwards at whim.

However, although the book has no fixed order, the activities in the first half are generally easier than those in the second half. The early pages encourage children to play with words, use alliteration, create riddles, select powerful words and describe and compare, using complex sentences. Later pages stimulate children to respond at greater length, explaining, directing, discussing, advising, making up stories and problem solving.

You do not need to do all the activities on each page at one sitting – the book has been deliberately designed to be re-read again and again, with more things to discover at each re-reading.

Extension activities

There are further suggestions of things to do related to each theme on pages 30 and 31. These, in turn, may prompt you to invent more activities of your own.

Talking and listening guidelines

There are suggested guidelines for how good speakers and listeners behave on page 32.

4

How to use this book

The four activities at the bottom of each double page provide starting points for conversation. Some invite children to discuss what they see and to use talk in an exploratory way. Others require a more formal response, using particular sentence structures and vocabulary. In some cases, sentence openers or models are given. These are merely suggestions for developing different types of sentence or vocabulary, such as comparatives or the use of time connectives (eg then, after), which will help children develop their talk beyond one or two word comments. You could also lead from a talking session into writing.

The pictures have been drawn so that there are usually many different possible responses – since an atmosphere of 'getting it right or wrong' will not encourage children to speak up. Children talk best when they feel relaxed and the people around them are interested in what they have to say. If children seem uncertain, begin by modelling a sentence structure (the text preceded by the speech bubble). Try to avoid firing questions that require one word answers. Use phrases such as 'tell me…', which invite more extended answers.

Talk partners

You may find it helpful to ask the children to 'think, share in a pair', before giving a response in front of a whole class. Working with a talk partner provides a chance to think together and sort out what might be said. It is also helpful if you can model a few possible responses, so that the children might listen and think carefully for themselves, before they rehearse their own reply in pairs and say it aloud in front of the class.

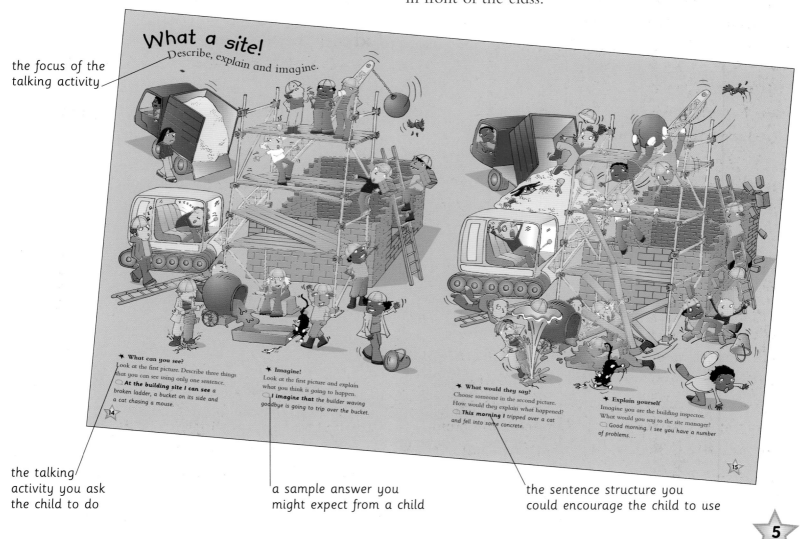

the focus of the talking activity

the talking activity you ask the child to do

a sample answer you might expect from a child

the sentence structure you could encourage the child to use

5

What is it like?
Play with words.

★ Invent riddles

Choose a creature, eg the tiger, and use adjectives to make up a riddle about it. Think about what it looks like and what it does. Who can guess your riddle?

💬 I am orange and black. My back is striped. My teeth are sharp.

★ Invent tongue twisters

Choose an animal and invent a tongue twister about it.

💬 The lazy lion laughed loudly at the lucky llama.

★ Invent powerful sentences

Choose an animal and use a verb to say what it does and an adverb to say how.

💬 The zebra **treads carefully**. The parrot **squawks loudly**. The snake **slithers silently**.

★ Crazy sentences

Choose an animal. Pretend it is human and can do the impossible.

💬 The owl wrote a book of recipes. The lion drove the bus to school.

Word building
Make compound words.

Compound words
Describe a compound word, eg shoelace, without using either part of the word. Who can guess it?

🗨 This is a length of cord you use to tie your trainers.

Syllable count
Say the compound words and count the syllables. Find two or three syllable words.

🗨 Toolbox has two syllables.

🗨 Rattlesnake has three syllables.

Rhyme it

Invent a rhyme as a clue for one compound word.
Who can guess the compound word?

🗨 Which compound word rhymes with cotton socks?
🗨 Matchbox!

Mix compound words

Make new compound words and give clues
for people to guess them.

🗨 These would help your toes to see more clearly.
🗨 Footglasses!

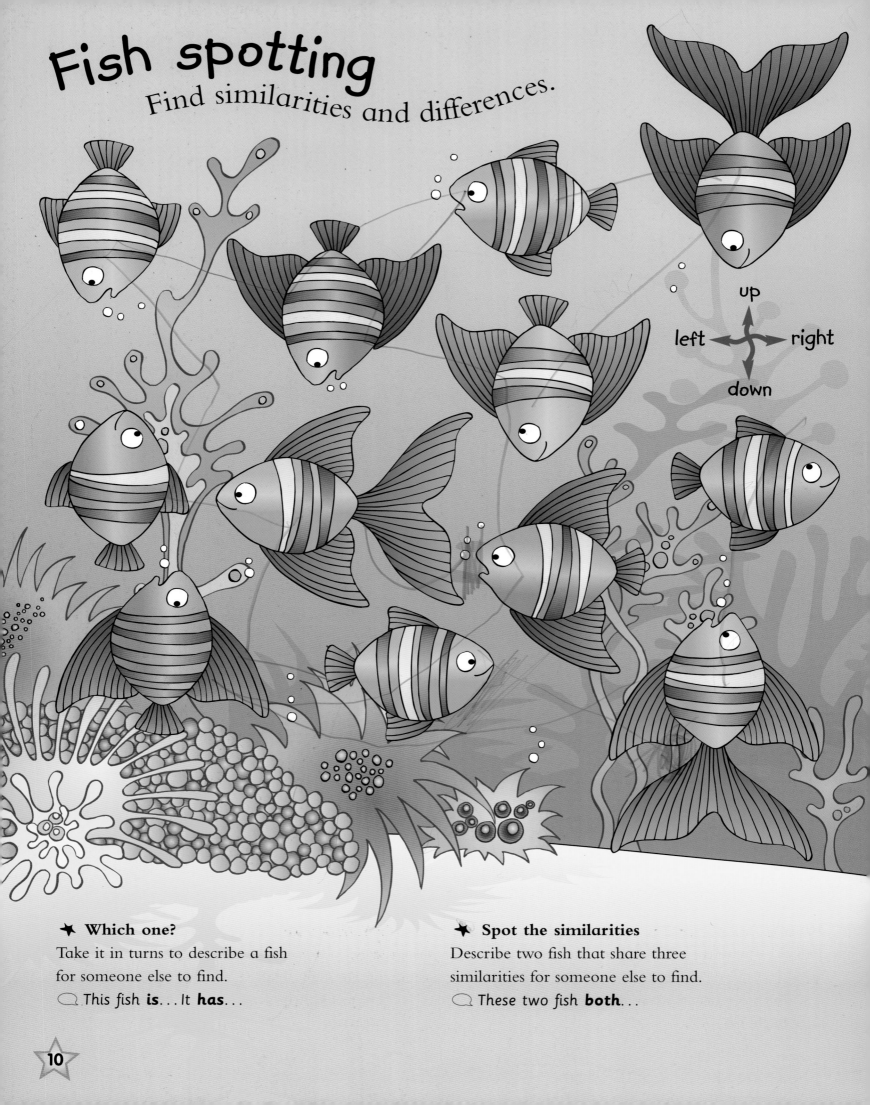

Fish spotting
Find similarities and differences.

up
left ↔ right
down

★ **Which one?**

Take it in turns to describe a fish
for someone else to find.

💬 This fish **is**... It **has**...

★ **Spot the similarities**

Describe two fish that share three
similarities for someone else to find.

💬 These two fish **both**...

★ **Spot the differences**

Choose two or three fish. Explain
how they are different.

🗨 These fish are different **because one**…
and **the other one**…

★ **Similarities and differences**

Point to two fish. Explain how they are similar
and how they are different.

🗨 These fish both… and… **but**…

Which popstar?
Use descriptive language and the past tense.

★ **Give clues**

Describe a popstar or an instrument for someone else to find.

○ **This popstar has** spiky pink hair.

○ **This instrument has** strings and a round body.

★ **Ask questions**

Take turns to ask a question about a person or an instrument for someone else to answer.

○ **Which popstar** is wearing sunglasses?

○ **Which instrument** do you play by shaking it?

★ **Spot the difference**

Choose two popstars and explain
the differences between them.

◯ **The differences between**...**and**...
are that...

★ **Tell me the past**

Choose a popstar and invent what they used
to do, using two sentences.

◯ **Before becoming famous, this popstar was**
a bricklayer in Muddletown. She built the lighthouse.

What a site!
Describe, explain and imagine.

★ **What can you see?**

Look at the first picture. Describe three things that you can see using only one sentence.

💬 **At the building site I can see** a broken ladder, a bucket on its side and a cat chasing a mouse.

★ **Imagine!**

Look at the first picture and explain what you think is going to happen.

💬 **I imagine that** the builder waving goodbye is going to trip over the bucket.

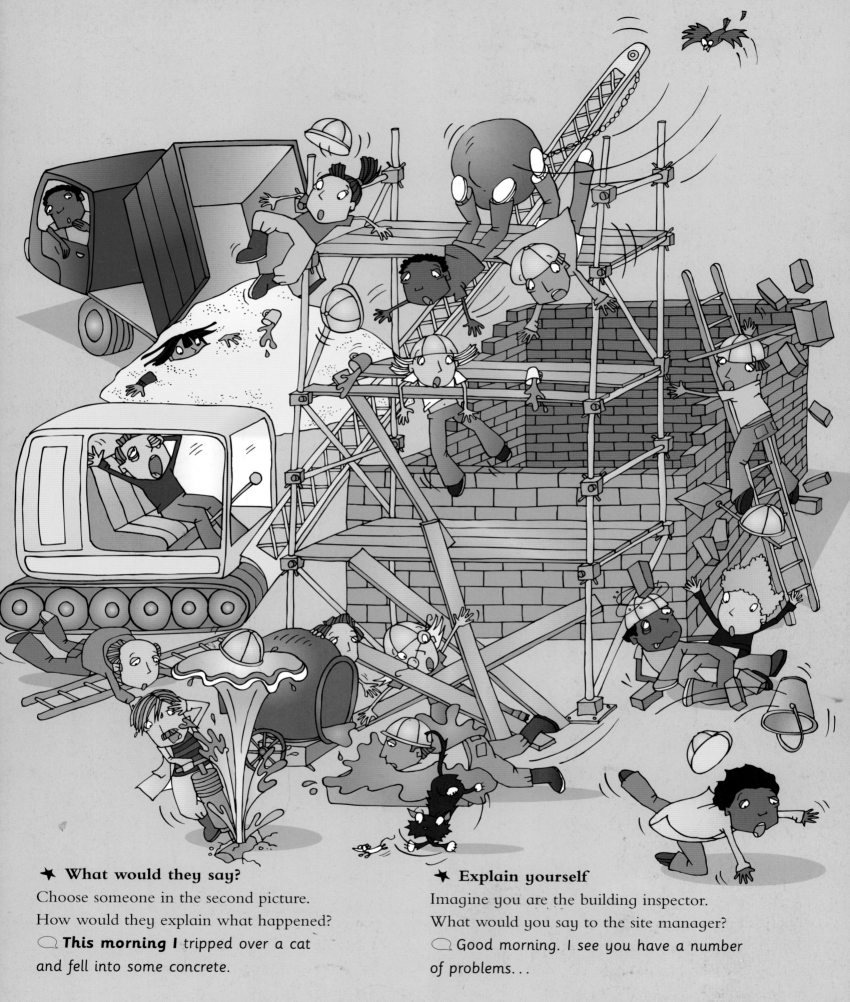

★ What would they say?

Choose someone in the second picture.
How would they explain what happened?

💬 **This morning I** tripped over a cat
and fell into some concrete.

★ Explain yourself

Imagine you are the building inspector.
What would you say to the site manager?

💬 Good morning. I see you have a number
of problems. . .

In the haunted house
Give directions.

★ **Hunt the skeleton**

Choose a skeleton and give three clues about where it is. Use words like below, above, beside, behind, near, next to and in between. Who can guess the skeleton you have chosen?

💬 Which skeleton **is above**... and **next to**...?

★ **Bring it alive**

Choose an object from the ghostly house. Pretend it comes alive.

💬 The chair **ran** up the stairs. The clock **cried** in the corner.

★ **Which way?**

Choose a skeleton or ghost and a far away room. Tell the skeleton or ghost how to get there. Use words like turn left, turn right, go along and keep going straight on.

💬 **To get to**... **you must**...

★ **Enter if you dare!**

Choose a child or an animal, eg the dog, and instruct it how to visit a room in the haunted house. Use powerful verbs and adverbs.

💬 **Creep past** the...
Run quickly through...

What happened next? Tell the tale.

★ **What's happening?**

Choose a set of pictures and explain what is happening.

◯ A boy buys a box and puts it on his shelf. He doesn't know that there is a dragon inside.

★ **What happened first?**

Invent a speech paragraph for each box. Practise the opening.

◯ Sally sat up in bed. She was certain that she had heard something downstairs. What on earth could it be?

★ **Invent a conversation**

Imagine you could talk to the different characters. What would you say to each other?

◯ Let's go and search the rest of the boat.

◯ No way! Someone might be hiding there.

★ **Finish it**

Tell the rest of the story. Introduce the action with 'suddenly' or 'at that moment'.

◯ At that moment Tim woke up. A bright light was shining...

What should they do?
Discuss and advise.

What's the problem?

Choose a situation in the picture and discuss what might happen.

◯ **Should** the giant hire the boy as his servant?

Should the boy decide not to work for the giant?

Reasons for?

Suggest reasons for one side of the argument.

◯ **One reason why** the giant should hire the boy as a servant is that he could help to protect the castle.

Reasons against?

Suggest reasons against the argument.

○ **On the other hand**, the giant might not hire the boy **because** he might trick the giant and steal his money.

At that moment…

Choose one character. Tell the story of what happens next using 'at that moment' to start.

○ **At that moment** the giant heard a sound from the forest. It was…

Don't do that!

Describe the dangers and make up rules.

What are they doing?

Discuss in pairs. Explain the problems you can see.

◯ **We think that**...

What will happen?

Trouble is brewing in Danger City! Take it in turns to suggest what might happen.

◯ **If** the girl goes too close to the dog, it might bite her!

You'll never guess…

Pretend you are one of the people in the city and tell a friend what you saw.

🗨 I was out shopping when I saw two people on rollerskates. What they didn't know was…

Make the rules

Make up some rules to make the street safer.

🗨 **Don't drop litter.**

🗨 **Don't leave dogs on their own.**

The story gang (1)

Pick ingredients for a story.

★ **Choose characters**

Pick and name your main characters and describe each of them in one sentence. Use three or more details.

💬 Jim had short, brown hair, wore an orange sweatshirt, jeans and trainers.

★ **Choose settings**

Pick a setting for the main adventure. Explain what dramatic event takes place there.

💬 Someone is kidnapped and held to ransom in the deserted house.

★ **Pick a story type**

Choose a story type from one of the books.

💬 **Warning**

Explain what will happen in your story.

💬 Jim is warned not to go into the deserted house but he does...

★ **Use connectives**

Practise using connectives by inventing lines for your story.

💬 **As soon as** Jim entered the house...

After	Immediately
As soon as	In the end
At that moment	Later on
Before	Meanwhile
Early one morning	Next
Eventually	Once
Finally	Since
First	So
However	Suddenly
If	Then
	When
	While

The story gang (2)
Organise your story.

Begin your story

Use this picture map to plan your story. Make up an exciting opening. Use a dramatic event.

💬 The old house stood empty until one day Jim passed by and thought that he heard a scream.

Build your character

How does your character feel? What does he or she say, do and think?

💬 Jim ducked down. I don't like the sound of that, he thought.

What happens next?

Tell the rest of the story to your partner or class, using connectives.

💬 Eventually, Jim plucked up courage. He crept up to the door...

End your story

At the end of your story show how the character has changed or what he or she has learned.

💬 I'm never going into empty houses again, thought Jim.

What's the matter?

Solve the problems.

Fish

Meat

★ **Watch out!**

Find a problem in the picture.

○ A dog is in the supermarket and it has taken some sausages.

★ **Solve it**

Discuss different ideas for solving the problem.

○ You could... You might...

If you... How about... Supposing...

28

★ Will it work?

Listen to some ideas and discuss their strengths and weaknesses.

◯ I like the idea... **because**... **but** you might find that...

★ Problem solvers

In pairs pretend that you are the supermarket manager and her assistant. Discuss how to solve the problems.

◯ Now Mr Williams, we have to stop those mice eating the cheese. What do you suggest?

Extension activities

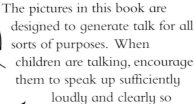
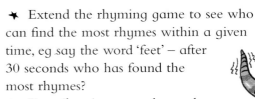

The pictures in this book are designed to generate talk for all sorts of purposes. When children are talking, encourage them to speak up sufficiently loudly and clearly so that everyone can hear and they do not have to repeat what they have said. Mirror standard versions back to them or ask them to complete what has been said, especially if it is fragmentary or over relies on gesture.

Give praise to those who use talk to organise roles in a group and ensure that everyone takes turns and is involved. Encourage children to reflect on feelings and relationships in stories and to explain processes and present information in a clear sequence with relevant details, supporting their views, leading to a well-defined conclusion.

Constant inventing, telling and retelling of stories as well as performing poems, using traditional language and expression, will help children to internalise basic patterns of narrative, including sentence patterns.

Use role-play and improvisation to explore stories and issues built around dialogue. Encourage children to discuss what makes performances successful. This can easily arise out of the pictures in this book by asking children to select characters or an event and act it out or discuss what happened retrospectively.

Pages 6-7 What is it like?

This double page provides practice in the ability to invent simple riddles, use alliteration, select powerful verbs and invent nonsense sentences.

★ You can use this spread in a variety of different ways. For instance, you might just simply spend time spotting the different creatures. Try describing them and seeing who can guess what you are looking at. Use positional language to add to the description, indicating where the creature is found – above, below, beside, and so on.

Pages 8-9 Word building

This double page looks at compound words. There are all sorts of other possibilities.

★ Make a list of other compound words. Use this to invent new compounds by adding bits from different words, eg football and handsome = footsome or handball.

★ Clap out names and see who can hear their syllable count, eg San-jay = 2 syllables.

★ Extend the rhyming game to see who can find the most rhymes within a given time, eg say the word 'feet' – after 30 seconds who has found the most rhymes?

★ Describe pictures and see who can guess what you are looking at.

Pages 10-11 Fish spotting

This double page is packed with fish! It can be used to practise simple description and discrimination, thinking about similarities and differences.

★ Use left/right/up/down to aid location.

★ Use the finer details, eg bubbles from mouth.

★ Invent jellyfish, using the same principles.

Pages 12-13 Which popstar?

This double page provides further practice in using precise descriptive language, asking questions, discussing differences as well as imagining what characters have been doing.

★ Invent names for each character and discuss what they might be like.

★ Choose characters to describe – what they are wearing, how they behave and how they speak.

★ Role-play the feedback in a pop competition, pretending that a character has just performed.

★ Which characters might be goodies and which could be baddies in a story?

★ Choose two characters and invent a conversation between them.

★ Choose a character and act out a simple situation, eg buying a carton of milk.

★ Role-play situations with different characters.

Pages 14-15 What a site!

This double page provides opportunities to use language in different ways – to describe, to imagine, explain and use dialogue.

★ Choose a builder – what might he or she be saying?

★ Put a builder in the 'hot-seat' and interview them about what has happened.

★ Invent a television news bulletin about the disaster.

★ Work in pairs and hold a discussion about what has happened.

Page 16-17 In the haunted house

This double page focuses on using instructional language to give directions.

★ Use the double page for description – describing the different rooms and what is happening in them.

★ Tell the story of what happens when the characters enter the house.

★ Recount a night spent in the haunted house.

★ Put a character in the 'hot-seat' and interview them about what happened when they spent a night in the haunted house.

Page 18-19 What happened next?

The groups of pictures provide opportunities for children to recount what has happened, is happening and what might happen next.

★ Use the pictures as a basis for storytelling. Provide story connectives that could be used, eg Once upon a time, one day, early one morning, so, next, when, while, after that, suddenly, without warning, at that moment, finally, in the end, eventually…

★ To encourage a simple pattern, ask the children to have:
- an opening
- a build up – in which the story begins
- a dilemma – where something goes wrong
- a resolution – which sorts out the problem
- an ending

★ Work in small groups to act out the scenes.

★ Continue the storyboards by adding in more pictures – before and after the three pictures shown. Use these as a simple way to aid plotting.

Pages 20-21 What should they do?

This double page sets up a host of different events which lend themselves to thinking about problems as well as imagining what might happen next. The idea of consequences lies at the root of storytelling.

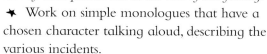

★ Work on simple monologues that have a chosen character talking aloud, describing the various incidents.

★ Explain what is happening and how each situation might be resolved.

★ In role as journalists, interview characters to discover what happened.

Pages 22-23 Don't do that!

This double page encourages children to describe events, using simple recounts. It is built around a series of possible dangers that need to be avoided. It could lend itself to all sorts of possibilities for talk, such as:

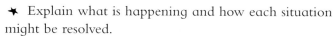

★ a recount given by a character telling a friend what happened;

★ an interview to television journalists about events;

★ a meeting between two characters who discuss how they are getting on;

★ an evil character trying to persuade a character to do something foolish;

★ using the picture as a basis for simple story making;

★ retelling events in diary format.

Pages 24-25 The story gang (1)

The pictures on this double page can be used as an imaginative way into story making. The picture provides basic ingredients to select from – various characters (goodies and baddies) and different settings.

★ Let children select one goodie, who will meet one baddie. Ask them to describe the characters and role-play with them in different situations, eg sitting on a bus together.

★ Encourage the children to say descriptive sentences that use detail to make the characters sound real.

★ Where will the story start and where will the action take place?

★ Invent descriptions for different settings.

★ Use question words – who, where, what, when, and how – to begin to flesh out a story idea:
- who are the characters?
- where are they?
- what goes wrong? (the dilemma)
- when is the story set? (past or present tense)
- how will it end?

★ With the children, scan books to add to the collection of story connectives. Practise sentences using these – and if children struggle, invent some together, initially modelling several examples.

Pages 26-27 The story gang (2)

The story picture map provides a chance for children to use it to invent their own story, with a simple structure.

★ Who is the main character? Where are they going? Why are they going? (Provide a simple task.) What route will they take? What awful event will befall them en route? (Bring the baddie into play!)

★ Think about how the story will end.

★ It is important to use the story connectives to help link events in the tale together.

★ Work out a story together as a class, then let children work in pairs to draw their own map, based on the spread and draw onto it their characters, and the main events. This can then be used as a basic plan to aid storytelling.

Pages 28-29 What's the matter?

This double page provides a good basis for pairs or groups to practise solving problems. Groups should divide up simple tasks, ensuring that:

★ they keep to a time limit;

★ they keep on task;

★ one person acts as scribe and notes ideas;

★ one person is in charge;

★ everyone has a fair turn at saying what they think. Logical solutions are welcome – but wacky ideas are also fun. Remember – the aim is for the children to share ideas and explain their reasons. This is about encouraging talking and listening – not about being 'right'.

How to be a good speaker and listener

When I speak, I need to:

* Be ready to ask people to explain ideas further.

* Respect ideas that I don't agree with.

* Add more points to a discussion and follow up points made by others.

* Make sure everyone is included in group discussions.

* Give reasons for my ideas: I think. . . because. . .

* Try to keep to the point.

* Use expression to make what I say sound interesting.

* Remember who I am talking with and how they might feel.

* Suggest ideas: What if. . .?

* Be ready to change my mind if I hear a good idea.

* Think of things that might be interesting or useful to say or add.

* Organise what I'm going to say with an introduction, the content and a conclusion.

* Include relevant details.

* Speak clearly, look at my audience and take turns.

* Organise the group into different roles for a discussion.

When I listen, I need to:

* Remember instructions and specific points.

* Show by my expression that I am interested in the speaker.

* Write down information or ideas that I might forget.

* Wait my turn before speaking.

* Look at the speaker, keep still and follow what is being said.

* Ask about anything I don't understand.